UNDER THE SEA

Clown Fish and other Coral Reef Life

Sally Morgan

QED Publishing

Copyright © QED Publishing 2008

First published in the UK in 2008 by
QED Publishing
A Quarto Group company
226 City Road
London EC1V 2TT

www.qed-publishing.co.uk

A catalogue record for this book is available
from the British Library.

ISBN 978 1 84538 949 9

Author Sally Morgan
Consultant Camilla de la Bedoyere
Editor Sarah Eason
Designed by Calcium
Picture Researcher Maria Joannou

Publisher Steve Evans
Creative Director Zeta Davies

Printed and bound in China

Picture credits
Key: T = top, B = bottom, C = centre, L = left, R = right,
FC = front cover, BC = back cover

Corbis Andy Rouse 21T, Kevin Schafer 20B, Lawson
Wood 18L, Nic Bothma/epa 11R,
Robert Yin 16-17, Visuals Unlimited 18C
Dreamstime 3, 6L, 7R, 10L, 16L
Getty Images David Nardini 5R
istockphoto 4L
Photolibrary Animals Animals, Earth Scenes 15B,
Mauritius Die Bildagentur Gmbh 10-11
Science Photo Library Georgette Douwma 17B
Shutterstock FC, 1, 2-3, 4-5, 6-7, 8-9, 8B, 11T, 12-13,
12-13C, 12B, 13T, 14-15, 15T, 18-19, 20-21, 22-23, 24

Words in **bold** can be found in the
glossary on page 22.

Contents

Coral reefs 4

Corals 6

Clown fish 8

Lionfish 10

Reef sharks 12

Sea slugs 14

Giant clams 16

Fan worms 18

Green turtles 20

Glossary 22

Index 23

Ideas for teachers
and parents 24

Coral reefs

Coral reefs look like beautiful underwater gardens. They are the home of many colourful animals, including fish, anemones, starfish and even sea snakes.

More than one million different types of animal live on coral reefs.

The Great Barrier Reef is made up of more than 900 islands.

Coral reefs are found in warm water. Some reefs grow in shallow water near land. Others are separated from the land by a stretch of water. The Great Barrier Reef in Australia is the world's largest reef. It is more than 2000 kilometres long.

Fish find plenty of food to eat on coral reefs.

Corals

Coral reefs are built by groups of tiny animals called hard **corals**. The corals have stony **skeletons**. When a hard coral dies, another coral grows on top of its skeleton. Over hundreds of years, the bony skeletons knit together to form the reef.

When a coral reef forms a circle, it is called an atoll.

Corals come in many shapes and colours. Hard corals can look like bubbles or trumpets. Some soft corals look like fans and gently sway in the warm waters.

Hard coral looks a little like a brain!

Small creatures can easily hide in colourful fan coral.

7

Clown fish

Sea anemones are animals that live on the reef. They have stinging **tentacles** that protect them from **predators**.

Most fish stay well away from sea anemones, but not the clown fish. The anemone's sting does not harm this brightly coloured fish, so it makes its home between the anemone's tentacles.

Clown fish are covered in a layer of slime to protect them from the anemone's sting.

Whole families of clown fish can live in one anemone.

The clown fish also gets its food from the anemone. It eats the anemone's leftovers, such as **shrimps**. In return, the clown fish cleans the anemone's tentacles and scares away other fish.

Lionfish

Darting around the reef is the lionfish. It has a striking, stripy body. This fish may look beautiful, but the spines on its **fins** give a painful sting.

Lionfish sometimes hunt together in groups to catch their **prey**.

Lionfish only use their stings for defence. If another animal threatens it, the lionfish does not need to swim away. It can simply point its deadly **spines** towards the enemy.

Lionfish spread out their fins to catch prey.

Lionfish are hunters. They corner prey with their large fins before swallowing them in one gulp.

Reef sharks

With its wide jaws and jagged teeth, the reef shark is a fierce hunter. Most sharks have a slim body and a powerful tail fin, perfect for gliding through water.

Octopuses, crabs and sea snakes are just some of the animals hunted by reef sharks.

Reef sharks have rows of deadly, jagged teeth.

Large flaps of skin make it difficult to spot the wobbegong shark on the seabed.

Sharks, such as the large black-tip reef shark and the small wobbegong shark, swim up and down the reef, on the lookout for fish and squid. They often hide in caves during the day and come out at night to hunt.

Sea slugs

Most sea slugs are the same size as garden slugs, but others are longer than a person's arm! Their bright colours warn other animals that they taste horrible.

Sea slugs eat animals that do not move, such as sea anemones and **sponges**. When a sea slug eats an anemone, it keeps the anemone's stings and puts them on its own back for protection!

The sea slug feeds on coral reefs.

Sea slugs scrape food off the reef with their sharp teeth.

Sea slug eggs are laid in the shape of a coiled ribbon.

Giant clams

Two huge shells protect
the giant clam's soft body.
It cannot move, so stays in
the same spot on the reef.

*If a clam senses danger,
it quickly closes its shells.*

To eat, the clam sucks in food through special tubes. It also gets food from tiny plants called zooxanthellae that live inside its body.

The oldest clams weigh about 300 kilograms – that is as heavy as three men!

The giant clam's bright colours come from the tiny plants that live inside it.

Fan worms

Fan worms are worms that live on coral reefs. They have an amazing crown of sticky, colourful tentacles. They eat any animals that get trapped on them.

If a fan worm senses movement, it slides back into its tube.

Fan worms are also called feather duster worms.

A fan worm attaches itself to a rock and builds a hard tube around its body for protection. The tube is made from tiny grains of sand that are stuck together with sticky **mucus**.

The Christmas tree worm
has bright tentacles that look
like a Christmas tree.

Green turtles

The turtle is an odd-looking animal. It has scaly skin and most of its body is covered by a tough shell. It has a large, beaklike mouth that it uses to graze on sea plants. The turtle is a **reptile**.

The female green turtle digs a hole in the sand and lays her eggs in it.

Green turtles are often seen swimming in shallow water near the coast.

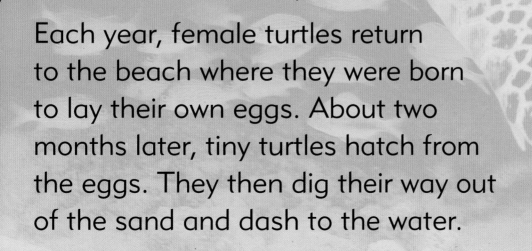

The newly hatched turtle makes its way to the sea.

Each year, female turtles return to the beach where they were born to lay their own eggs. About two months later, tiny turtles hatch from the eggs. They then dig their way out of the sand and dash to the water.

Glossary

atoll a circular coral reef

coral an animal from which coral reefs are built

coral reef a group of hard rocks made of coral

fin the part of a fish used to swim and steer

mucus a sticky substance made by animals

predator an animal that hunts other animals

prey an animal that is hunted by other animals

reptile an animal with scaly skin that lays eggs

shrimp a small sea creature with a shell around its body

skeleton the framework of bones supporting the body

spine a long, sharp point

sponge a soft-bodied sea animal

tentacle a long, armlike limb of a sea creature. It is used for feeling and holding, and sometimes for stinging

Index

anemones 4, 8, 9, 15
atoll 6, 22

black-tip reef shark 13

Christmas tree worm 19
clams 16, 17
clown fish 8, 9
coral reefs 4, 5, 6, 8, 13,
     15, 16, 18, 22
corals 6, 7, 22
crabs 12

eggs 15, 20, 21

fan coral 7
fan worms 18, 19
feather duster worms 18
fish 4, 5, 8, 9, 10, 12, 13

giant clams 16, 17
Great Barrier Reef 4, 5
green turtles 20, 21

hard corals 6, 7

lionfish 10, 11

octopuses 12

reefs 4, 5, 6, 8, 13, 15,
     16, 18, 22
reef sharks 12, 13
reptiles 20, 22

sea anemones 4, 8, 9, 15
sea slugs 14, 15
sea snakes 4, 12
sharks 12, 13
shrimps 9, 22
soft corals 7
sponges 15, 22
squid 13
starfish 4

turtles 20, 21

wobbegong shark 13
worms 18, 19

Ideas for teachers and parents

- Encourage children to think up funny stories about the clown fish and its life on the coral reef.

- Look at an atlas to find the Great Barrier Reef in Australia. Find out where other coral reefs are around the world.

- Visit an aquarium that has a coral reef exhibit.

- Look at some of the many websites that feature coral reefs. Some have webcams set up underwater so that children can watch the reef animals.

- Make a collage of a coral reef. Take a large piece of white paper and draw an outline of a reef, using the photos in this book for inspiration. Look through old magazines and cut out any pictures of fish, sea anemones and other reef animals. Stick these on the outline to make the reef colourful.

- There are many partnerships on coral reefs, such as the clown fish that lives with sea anemones, and the zooxanthellae that live with corals and giant clams. Find out more about these relationships and how each partner benefits.

- Coral reefs are under threat from pollution, global warming and even divers collecting tropical fish for the aquarium trade. Find out more about these threats and what can be done to protect the reefs.

- Make a wordsearch using the reef-related vocabulary in this book.